why
isn't
everybody
dancing

Donated to
SAINT PAUL PUBLIC LIBRARY

S0-ABR-980

why
isn't
everybody
dancing

MAARA HAAS

TURNSTONE PRESS

Copyright © 1990 Maara Haas

Turnstone Press
607-100 Arthur Street
Winnipeg, Manitoba
Canada   R3B 1H3

Turnstone Press gratefully acknowledges the assistance
of the Canada Council and the Manitoba Arts Council.

Cover illustration: Steve Gouthro, brush and ink drawing.

This book was printed by Hignell Printing Limited
for Turnstone Press.

Printed and bound in Canada.

All rights reserved. No part of this work covered by the
copyright hereon may be reproduced or used in any form
or by any means—graphic, electronic or mechanical—
without the prior written permission of the publisher.
Any request for photocopying of any part of this book
shall be directed in writing to the Canadian Reprography
Collective.

Canadian Cataloguing in Publication Data

Haas, Maara

    Why isn't everybody dancing

    Poems.
    ISBN 0-88801-146-6

I. Title.

PS8565.A28W49 1990   C811'.54   C90-097047-2
PR9199.3.H22W49 1990

to those who listened and cared:

Fred Kerner, Joyce Dunn, James Hutchison, Kurt Haas,
Betty Milway, Larry Thomas, Ronald Lightbourne and
the Ministers of Culture, Bermuda; Dudley Fubler,
Lloyd Haas, William Zuill, Helen Massie Douglas,
Gordon McRae, Josephine Darrell Büch, David Arnason,
Charles Wilkins, Patrick Lane, Cora Taylor

and to the Manitoba Arts Council whose financial
support made this work possible

my thanks.

special thanks:

to Mrs. Lois Brown-Evans, M.P., J.P.
for the quotation from *Bermuda's Heritage*;
Margaret Carter for the excerpt from "Prospect Square"
(*Longtales*, the Bermuda Writers' anthology, 1982);
and to Ronald Lightbourne for perspectives from
"Which Way Bermuda" (*The Bermudian*,
anniversary issue, 1984).

acknowledgements

I have taken, modified and, in some instances, dramatized material from the following sources: *Chained on the Rock* by Cyril Outerbridge Packwood, *Bermuda's Crime & Punishment* by Terry Tucker, *Slavery in Bermuda* by James E. Smith, *The Rich Papers, 1615-1646* (Bermuda Trust) by Vernon E. Ives, *The Dark World of Witches* by Eric Maple, *The Listener, The Royal Gazette, The Bermuda Sun, The Bermuda Gazette and Advertiser* and the Bermuda Library Archives.

special acknowledgement

for permission to incorporate references in the fictionalized "Last Will and Testament" from *Bermuda Settlers of the 17th Century* by Julia E. Mercer (Baltimore, Maryland: the Genealogical Publishing Co. Inc., 1982).

To protect the privacy of those involved in the "Slave Wall" and the "Last Will and Testament," names have been changed and places, dates and situations altered.

this book is dedicated
to the living memory
of my daughter lani

to my sister jean sinkwich

and my adopted daughter
diane cardno

who knew the meaning
of the dance

contents

i   long distance

the phone rings

i hold a seashell murmuring atlantis
sunstone of a generating force
flowing sound waves

                on a bend of light
                the island rises

sleepwalker
treading without motion
layers of heat hallucinating ocean
my image rims the white afternoon

salt spray blisters my mouth
the dense odour of marine kelp
              overripe bananas
seeping my clothes   my hair

and i see my backward shadow
leaning front street's old world balcony

open ocean yachts   the edge of sail
like fin of phantom shark
splicing the sky

again
down south street road
i run for shelter in a phone booth

torrential rain
pelting the roof of my head
with the soft staccato of
broken oleander blooms

at the slope of the road
a barefoot bermudian
is dancing

he waves to me
through a blur of glass

my heart dances to the
pattern of his feet
breaking the dialtone

unexpected as torrential rain
your absence inundates the space where
i have placed you

your death was a lobotomy
a part of my brain cut away

for a long time after i hid your clothes
your personal belongings

arms legs torso eyes
pieces of you

in secret places
bureau drawers jewellery boxes filing cabinets

arranging rearranging trying to put trying to
put things together
trying to put you together

there were signs of life a breathing i swear it
in the folds of the dress you once inhabited
the windsong of your silk scarf
pale but clear on the dying air

i chanted words of adoration
calling on Osiris and Teta
the waters of heaven the scarab of the sun

behold Lani cometh forth on this day
in the form exact of a living soul

there was no resurrection

now everything i put away in proper places
reappears somewhere else

now people who used to talk to me
in triplicate voices
from a tristan / isolde echo chamber

simply walk through me

i trace the warmth of your aura
ring of fire   fire of hoarfrost
on the windowglass

pressed against the glass wall
        glass wall
        between the
mute living and the speaking dead

perfectly poised against the feeder
his open beak brimming birdseed
        a frozen starling

congregations of sparrows
fluttering above him
        mid air

meditating on the stalks of pencils
growing in a flowerpot

matching the whorls of my finger-
tips to the whorled patterns of my
oak desk

emanating trees   rain forests
fern poems   earthstone images

conjuring up your voice from
old snapshots
greyed penumbra of events   places

all that you touched in passing

          eating a pear

or tonight for no apparent reason
crushing the pear   a human skull
between my hands

upstaged by death
a newcomer
joan crawford   always professional
always a lady
made death her protégé   her lover

one late summer's eve
the moon in closeup
she knelt down in a bed of roses
tearoses   her favourite flowers

guillotined their heads with garden shears
to avenge the living

          i shall have to watch myself
more carefully
from now on

you are at the front door   winter
weighed down warmly in the aztec poncho
we took turns wearing

red leather boots   your small red purse
butterfly brooch   bird   or wild flower

this wednesday   a white anemone
pinned to the strap

                    and your voice lilting upward
                    hello   it's me   Lani

coiled in your pain (please don't let me die)
you confessed reluctantly   stemming your pride

                    your secret fears

waiting for the bus to work   seeing yourself
collapsed on the pavement (help   someone
anyone
i can't lift my body from the platform)

i am waiting to tell you the news of the day

the bright bermuda kerchief you wore
in hospital to cover your frail hair
isn't lost   yes   i have it

Kurt agrees we are going to need a new tent
will our camping trip be Carman or Hecla
maybe we could study the map after supper

your name follows me through the house
                    but you are absent

i phone you at work   you are not there

i call your apartment 85 rings
                    no answer

i keep returning
to our favourite meeting place
coffee and crullers
                    the corner table
                    by the window

waiting   waiting   watching
                    you don't appear

i am writing you this letter
as a last resort   a last hope
hoping to reach you

where are you Lani

it rained that day at the bog
in my memory
the kind of day
marking good friday

i   carrying the urn
hardlathed   inanimate

Kurt pushing a passage
to the musky water's edge
waterlogged brambles
bulrushes   fireweed

your ashes   pulverized marble
sifting between his hands

       by some metamorphosis
       a scattering of bone beads
       clinging to the underside
       of thick rainwet grass
       as if growing lily of the valley
       sudden
       in our path

       i was a child of water
       where i appeared i fed the air
       green   succulent
       a flowering of flesh

       my ribs dividing the red sea
       of my blood
       opened an oasis

tired caravans
lay down their bones beside me
desert horses stopped in wonder
      drank me in and were restored

    you loved the northern solitudes
where you said if you lived forever
with time to spend every minute
counting the pine trees

their numbers would still race
ahead of you

      never to be reconciled
we think later
of all the things
we might have done   undone
too late knowing

you would have salvaged
the scruffy pine
thrown into the ashcan
at the train station

      we lie in our berths   sleepless
the blind eyes of small towns
illuminating briefly
the thin outline of your other self
stencilled against the sky

the smooth hearse of the midnight run
taking us out of the nowhere
to which you now belong

toward the end
i waited for the flood within me
to rush
the wall around my heart
while i looked on
a witness to my drowning
violent   merciful

but it came slowly
my strength easing from my fingertips
my tongue thirsting
scorched by desert sun
in a floating landscape

>   *myself a green oasis*
>   *fading*
>   *as i crawled toward it*

you are reading kingsley's waterbabies
a faery tale for land babies
obedient feet   sturdy shoes
earthbound
your eyes searching out
a place   a distance
i cannot see

            in the way objects diminish living entities
cradle   wedding ring   coffin
assume priority

transient faith an insect
on the eye of buddha
the permanence of icons absolute

        your little girl likeness in a garden chair
pigtails   chubby knees
a dazed bee bumbling your flowered pinafore
receding   disappear

only the garden chair remains

parting
i made the sign of the cross over you

earth

air   *fire*

water

choose your element

ii   slave wall

... slave quarters and old drystone slave
walls can be seen meandering along country
lanes. ...

the visitor's complete
bermuda guide 1973

eight trybe roads interlace
the black heart of the island

drystone walls porous as decaying teeth
heaving inward   define the lazy pattern

of their course   push back relentless
pampas grass reclaiming plantations

raw tobacco   sugar cane   slave quarters
built three hundred years ago

the earth there
is the colour of pulpy rotting pumpkin
or dried blood
though no blood was spilled officially

        hamilton   smiths   pembroke
        paget   southampton   sandys
        warwick   devonshire

these are the arteries the dried out rivers
of a land unreconciled to its beginnings

salt raker slaving the bahamas
flesh eaten acid to the bone

dockyard convict slave
in typhus holds

white woman birthing black child
lashed to a public whipping post

pilfering thieving slave
adulterous slave

suffering the pillories of puritan corrections

ears cropped and nailed   nostrils slit
heads impaled on gallows' island

blaspheming slave   forehead branded B
tongue seared with heated irons

sea venture derelict
lifted from the devil's pocket
triangle

        float and shimmer
        this haunted ground

one among them
balances above her head
the candelabra of a life force
greater than her own
a part of her   miraculous   unscathed untouched
by the after flame

one
mortared in a wall of words
reads my epitaph

      mimicking life
i will rise up with the slave-wall dead
on christmas day
to join the gombey dancers on parade

fierce in the armour of their thickly painted masks
slashed scarlet   violent yellow   head a pyramid
plumed with flower   ribbon   feather ornaments

dance out life's contortions
dance to the singing pulse of wrists and ankles
dance to the rhythmic chanting of my chains

dance to the beat   the heartbeat of gomba

breaking down slave walls

why
isn't
everybody
dancing

up and down and over
country roads bridle paths jungle footpaths
the length of the island

i followed a crinoline lady
in a starched white gown
so stiff and smooth she could have been
hewn from rock salt

her velvet tasselled sedan chair
was borne by a slave
and another shouldering her wardrobe trunk

ribboned mantle taffeta
madeira silver lace
necklaces brooches amethyst pearls and gold
satined dancing shoes

i am going to the grand ball at st. george's
                    she said

her eyes
forever looking to the past

staring at me from the back of her head

Runaway NED guinea born, 5'9" slender made remarkable blacke, is pitted with smallpox a cast to his left eye, good teeth and can work a little at the carpenters business a caulker by trade, speaks good English, and is supposed to be gone off in the ELIZA fr boston or in the sloop st. john fr halifax as he caulked on board both these vessells
captured slave
the property of nathan trimminham
paget parish
july 17, 1771

who lived in that limestone house
small windowed like a cell

backlane alleyway of night voyeur cockroaches
rats and toilet waste

the house foreshadowed by the great mansion
greek balustrades
quaker hedges trimmed to conformity
buttery rooftops descending rain
with the quietness of bayou moss

were they lovers
coupled in nakedness between the innocence
of children
ankles shackled   wedged into stone

what were their thoughts dawn quickening
the turn of the outside key in the door

their keeper's footsteps
heavy and sure

POSTPONED SALE
ON ACCOUNT OF BAD WEATHER

On Friday next, the 18th instant
At three o'clock
Mrs. Bristow's near Walfingham Bay
Several Negroes, viz:

Ruthy   about 40 years old
Asia   38 ditto
Straw   20 ditto
Aletta   55 ditto
Rose Ann   12 ditto

Besides 1 old Musket, 2 brass Compasses a ewe Lamb, 1 Porcelain Chamber Pot New 3 pr. Silver Buckles, 1 cedar Chest all Household Furnishings being part of the Estate of the very Honorable
Capt. Gillbert Stovell

Hamilton
March 4, 1816

old sally bassett lay awake night after night
thinking up poison plots
                    to set her grievance right

ratsbane creviced in the louvered kitchen door
one whiff her mistress smelling it
                    would of a sudden stop her breath

one dose of manchineel to spice the black bean soup
she saw her master writhing in a spasm
                    quick to seal his death

june the sun burns fire neither ocean breeze
nor rain can slake

the flame and body heat of sally bassett
burning at the stake

having no memory of it passing strangers
on the common street
                    are heard to say

man it's hot
looks like we've got a scorching
                    sally bassett day

TO BE SOLD AT AUCTION

On Monday next, the 16th instant
At ten o'clock
At his Dwelling House
All household effects to include
1 sailver headed cane & sailver
Mugge without a mark, two Joint
Stools, 3 armed Chairs, Spinning
Wheels and 1 Candell Cup etc.

ALSO

A valuable young Mulatto Woman, who
for the space of nearly ten years has
done the whole work of a Family, eight
persons Washing and Ironing and is a
good Sick Nurse & a strong Field Worker

ALSO
an excellent Horse

St. George's
May 12, 1814

black beck would not be halved
would not give her firstborn

        into slavery

spit on the midwife
spit the swaddling clothes

        of bondage

when her water broke
like the stream of jordan

        hallelujah

she humped the coral sand

delivered child

alive and screaming to be

        cut free

and tenderly
        she buried him there

january 17, 1784, Runaway from the subscribr the bermuda gazette and advertiser an Indian wench named HAGAR, her person midling tall & slender, yellowith complexion, lantorn jawed has lost most of her fore teeth so appearing little drawn to the mouth when she laughs by haughty movement of head showing much vanity the same guilty of BRAVE APPAREL. Any person carrying her off the islands will bee by law persecuted and will answer to master R. Long of hogg bay

i saw a witch hanged in the square

i wore my sabbat dress
      the day was fair

they sealed her mouth with grass
they tied her hands
      her feet were bare

Come butter come
come butter come
Saint Peter stands at thy gate
waiting for a buttered cake
Come butter come

her breasts were open like a whore

her thighs were open
      where the cambric tore

i saw the devil's claw
      imprinted there

the witnesses all swore as one

SHE bade me with a heifer lie
SHE put the fever in my loins
     she willed it done

SHE mixed a poultice straw and mud
to draw the poison from a boil
what healing struck me deaf and blind
     the spell she spun

          Bury deep and smooth
          around
          a pair of scissors
          near the ground
          to keep a SeaHag
          from thy door

          Steel shall cut
          and stab her sore
          and she shall trouble
          thee no more

they swam the witch to save her soul

she did not drown
            she floated sound and whole

that day the butter would not churn

her neighbour's mare she
            birthed a stillborn foal

                    Plant of sessile,
                    rue and dill
                    tye with ribbon
                    to thy windowsill

                    and surely
                    thou shalt break
                    the Witch's Will

twelve women probed her hidden parts

eyelids armpits womanhood
    the web of hair

twelve women pins and needles
    searched her out

searched out Sathan's incubus to
    catch him dreaming
      unaware

inside the witch's mouth they found a sore

the duggs that imps and demons
        suck upon

the bloodless spot sustained by sin
        the secret place
she let the devil in

Father Son and Holy Ghost
nail the devil to the post
thrice i strike with holy crook
once for Wodin
once for God
and once for Luk

i heard the dead boughs of the tree

crack their knuckles as
    her neck swung free

i heard the clacking women's tongues
spilling pods of
    false black ebony

i saw a witch hanged innocent

the devil waited till her
      soul was spent

she wore my face she wore
      my name
i in another image took no
      hurt or blame

Hare Hare God send thee caire
i am in a hare's likeness
just now

but i shall soon be
in a woman's likeness
this i vow

january 24, 1784 Runaway slave a negro
Woman named TABITHA, bermuda born
twenty two years of age, five feet high, very
black and lusty has lately had the smallpox,
probable she is harboured by some of the negro
neare spanish point, as she came from that
place last seen

obediah humphrey
port royal

i shook the hand of christ
his hand was black

the whip of slavery lay across his back

he planted freedom's seed
it died   it was reborn

bermuda's passion flower
          bearing thorn

first glimpse of dawn
the day of liberation
susannah wakes to meet the lord
scrubs scrubs scrubs her body
till her skin
glistens

o wash me in the blood of the lamb
o baby jesus wash away my sin

nine years in servitude
she's earned her freedom suit

flannel jacket osnabrig   cotton lined
coarse cotton dress
laid out in her lap
like bridal finery

her first free sunday
walking to the church
carries her whaleskin shoes
new   untried

like feast day chickens
nesting under each arm
right shoe at her right hand
left shoe at her left

pilgrim to the promised land

Formerly the property of captain george evans a negro wench CRETIA FERNANDEZ, absconded wth one holland cheese and one pair of shoes wort five shillings, short stature and stoute made All persons are hereby forbid harbouring else employing her. Masters of Vessels are forbade taking her of these islands on pain of strict most rigour of the law being enforced against them. A reward of four dollars will bee given to any person that will secure her or deliver her to symour bullock

sandys parish
march 13, 1805

john stephenson

methodist missionary
was imprisoned in this jail six months
and fined fifty pounds
for preaching the gospel of jesus christ
to african slaves and captive negroes

st. george's —— bermuda
june 1801

so inscribed with a knife
on the cedar planking of
my cell floor

Runaway about eight months ago, a negro girl
name LETTICE, about 13 years of age 4 feet 6
or 8 inches high, a likely countenance, thik lips
and bold face, supposed to be harboured in
pembroke. A reward of thirty dollars will be
paid to any person who brings her or from any
goal or workhouse where she may be found

lieut. josua brigden
hamilton parish
august 9, 1834

In the name of God Amen.

The ffirst day of Aprill in the yeare of our Lord Christ Six hundred Seventy and ffoure I Malachi Leabourne being about 84 years but of perfect memory God be Praised, doe make and ordaine this my Last Will and Testament.

Item I doe guie and bequeath vnto my eldest Sonne Ephram & my Daughter Abigail between them tthree shares of Land in Paget & the Dwellings to the Land belonging wch shall bee held in lease for their lifetime & made to my Wife's Estate in yearly rent viz: 250 lbs. tobacco & 2 capons & a turkey cock 'at the usual time of division' falling on the Ffeast of Saint Michaels Archangel.

Item on the disposition of a Mulatto girl Keziah she bee devised first to my youngest Sonne Thomas. If Thomas die before he hath wife or issue the girl goes to Sonne John and if he hath no wife or issue my GrSonne Charles shall inherit her.

Moreouer I guie vnto my G^rSonne Charles the sloop Marrea anchored in these ilands, the storehouse was built by me at the shoreside wth 8 ft. of ground privligis, 2 payers silk hose scarcly worn, 1 silver spoon my initials on it engraved & my privit store in hold 40 lb. Holland Cheese 6 gallons Salat Oyle, 1 cask Biskit, 1 barrell China Tea 1 firkin Butter & 4 gallons Aquavitae, to bee replenishd 5 yrs. he cumme of age, myne Executor Mr Aaron Frobisher and Josh. Sculloe Merchant liuing in England tto see the same deliured. If GrSonne Charles die before he inharrit all monys to stores shall stay wth the Honorable Company shares gowing vnto my Wife's Estate.

Item let it bee known that by agreement wth the Gentlmen privitly named I renounce all claims to a neger boy Tome ownd and shared between us wch we did freely giue to Sir Symon Knight by deed of gift in considerashin of fayvers receivd . . . to hold & to use the aforesaid Tome fr his own & his heirs & administraytrs ffor the terme of 99 yeares.

In Addishin I guie my Midle Sonne John aforesaid my olde Crosse Saw, 1 Beam & Scale wth leaden waights, 1 bottome of a Cedar Canoe not sea worthy but still usefull on wch to dress fish, 2 Woodin Blocks for pressing cassava root as mayk bread flour, my Brass Compasse & ttwenty sheares (500 accers) plantacion, Fruit Vines, Mangrove & Tobbaco that bee the ppropertie of my Trybe.

Item I guie vnto my youngest Sonne Thomas aforesaid, the goodes receivd by me in marketible commodaty from slaves sold: Augustine for 700 waight Salt Beef, Megge, Israell & Hagar for 18,000 lbs. Merchents Suger, the slave Jacob dew 3 pds. In Hand & 600 waight Salt Beef. Him Saul for Ambergris & the neger Polydone sold for a Small Boat wth Oars, Rudder & Sayles & from my personall effekts he may choose my gold Beer Bowl or my Blacke Suitt & gud Girdel answerable to my Suitt.

To my Kinswoman Luella Grimditch, a Single Woman, I guie the mahogony Table missing 1 leaf, the blacke Milche Cow ffifteene pounds Sterling & my second best Bible for her evening prayyrs & the deed by wch she has the liberty of the South side of the Mansion what corne and potatoe was planted.

Imprimis to my trusty Brother Dudley I liue 40 shillings a yeare that he ouersee the Pit Trapps as keep the Ratts from the Turkey Corne devoured & the same he ouersee s^{ch} good invoyced: 2 boxes oranges, lymons, ffiggs packtt in cedar board, 1 cedar cask Indigo, 7 Buts (large casks) & 4 Hoggshead (smaller casks) Tobaco to Wm Bassett Esquire on any vessell touching port Fulmouth, Plymouth, Dartmth fr seruices receivd that him, my Brother Dudley bee payd in addishin my parcell of Land from the Sea to the Onion Patch & the capturd neger Virgil to run before his horse.

To shee my Wife Honora I guie and bequeath the remainder of my Estate, the Land, Slave Dwellings, Outhouses & all other Edifices, the Mansion & all household stuffes save the mahogony Table missing 1 leaf, & the remaining Bonde Servants unaccounted as well the neger woman Susette and if she (Susette) hath a child, my Wife owns that too, so long as shee doth keep my name and so long as shee lives during her Gud Behaviour but if shee doth marry, May God Forbid, 2/3 of her Estate shall bee divided among living heirs more Worthy.

Item that a cask of Wine bee bought for the funeral.

Item to those who help to beare me to the Grave, each a Pair of Gloves.

Item tthree Mourning Rings each for my Wife, my Eldest Sonne and Daughter.

'In witness of the promisses
I haue subscribed my name and sett my seale
the day and yeare ffirst aboue written
I commend my soule vnto Allmighty God
my Maker and my merciful Ffather in
Jesus Christ who hath redeemed me by his
precious Blood from the bondage of
Sinn and Sathan from Hell and Everlasting
damnation and hath obtained for me
the forgiunesse of my sinnes
peace with God and I trust
everlasting Blessednesse in his
heauenly kingdome.'

Malachi Leabourne X

Witnesses

Barnard Trott
The mark *⁚* of Samuel Stow

Humphrey Tucker Martial

if you walk softly
the hardened roads
    once dragged by chain

the earth shifts

and the trees reach out to
clasp you like a living thing
    being drowned

a man hanged himself on
trybe road

the slow muffled heartbeat of
african drums
    calling him home

iii   poems out of exile

bermudian cabdriver
smelling out a fare at the flatts
smiles at the woman in the watermelon
pink and green lady windermere straw hat
elton john shades screening the sun
long cotton skirts unwinding
white and skinny as flamingo legs

good lord is it really me

cabdriver

and you're the writer from can-idda
recognize you from the newspapers
mid ocean   bermuda sun

come lookin' for a slave wall that ain't there
that's some story

                    throwing out a long line
                    to snag the thought
                    ending every thought
                    with an mmmmmmm
                    thinkin' about it thinkin' about it
                    believin' don't come easy

how long you stay this time
sees how your grandson still fishin'
sure like fishin'

no luck today
fish thinkin' smart on friday
smart you let the fish be
havin' yerself a lazyday bermuda picnic
want to be watchful under them palmetto
'merican tourist he's sittin' the same spot
coconut he drop hisself dead centre
put the misery in the poor man's head
took him fast to brendan hospital
        all the way from can-idda
        lookin' for a slave wall ain't there
        mmmmmmm
        you cookin' up another story now

woman

well   since you ask
there's this story swimming in my head
far back so far you can't remember
long before slavery times
and i'm meeting with a blind sailor
sometimes going by the name of GOD

he does his job   he makes the earth
he's just bone tired aching for a world of rest

glances round and finds a piece of ocean
he overlooked
where he can fish
and sleep with one eye open

day and night he casts his fishing line
to catch a human sinner on the bait

sharptooth barracuda businessman
hooks on the shiny buckle of the man's shoe
thieving moray curled up in a ball
hit him with a hatchet
catching him on edge
land or ocean shark slicker   easy catch
poor eyesight does him in

after who knows how many million years
GOD quits the boat
gives up fishing when his son
takes on the nets

and here's bermuda where the islands join
shaping the giant fish-hook
GOD left behind

          some story eh

mmmmmmm

before chemicals bleached out the colours of the world
my grandmother whitened her petticoats with blueing

galvanized metal washtubs
hard water

small ceremony dipping the chalky cube electric blue
lifting the cheesecloth like an arcade artist

manipulating a clawed crane to bite the glittering
grand prize a two buck pocketwatch

her memory in the stilled waters of my dreams
is flung up on the waves' sudsy opalescent foam
streaked indigo

sky a separate island edged amethyst and cobalt blue
floats the sunbleached beaches whitening the horizon

my mind my pores are stained blue
the colour of my grandmother's blueing eyes

the devil he come to dinner
he wear bermuda shorts
he wear a silk shirt stars and stripes and dollar bills
he wear front street alligator shoes
he wear a neon button in his lapel
flashing free trade free trade
you don' look away
you seein' blind

the devil he say   you   *boy*
give me a good black woman to pleasure me
give me that corner of the island
hell needs another military base
the devil's playmates need more slotmachines
the devil's currency in god we trust
you play the devil's game you shoot the devil's dice

the devil he come to dinner
he got some big appetite
he swallow your beaches he swallow the ocean he
swallow your children   he clean his teeth with a bayonet

the devil he say   you   *slave*
spit when i say spit
kneel when i say kneel beg when i tell you beg

everyone polite to the devil

the devil he leave fat gratuities

archaeological finds in a cove
a plastic spoon
a tin of amsdel beer
clumps of seaweed

a balding sea crone picnicked here
her skin i imagine was pocked like
this black crater of volcanic rock the
labyrinths of driftwood turned to
stone eaten by salt and silence wild
island cats circled round her drawn
out by the raw squid odour of her
fresh sea breath

maybe she gummed the plastic spoon
found no pleasure in it suckled on the
tin of beer and humming softly sat
down to brush her twigged hair
leaving clumps of torn dry seaweed
everywhere

good mornin' ah seh to lizard
him lookin' sleepy   not movin' hisself

him blink his eye:
dat tourist down dere
jus' waitin' fer lizard do somet'ing cleva
so lizard obligin' when tourist
      him come by

tourist him starin' starin' starin'
lawd lawd him cry
you knows wad i seen
dat lizard turnin' grey to green

        an' why you not so sweetie
sweetie wid me ah seh

lizard him laughin' ha ha
gwan' yu ways fren'
you an' me don' need preten'

i surprise myself
each time i touch his cheek

the texture is cork
sucked dry by sun
salt tears evaporated

he is cork
floating dead oceans
from a time remembered
i will not admit to

i would sleep with him
my cheek against his cheek

playing mermaid
not of the land or sea

and he would leave me
my fin severed from my body

the sandstrands of my hair
consumed by wind

to lie this beach or any other

wary of midnight anglers
gentleman Trott built a wall around this pool
a hundred years ago

and later for a small price of admission
provided free fishing line and bait
for anyone behaving civilly

dangling the bait for the pleasure in it

watching the play of pretty parrotfish
medusa octopus and moray eel

trying to rouse a loggerhead turtle
his eyes hooded cataracts of patience
quietly amused

in the game of fisherman
and turtle camouflaging russet stone

       an agate scooped up from the sea
the pool flowed darkly secretly underground
unwelcome light seeping through the ribs of sky
cavern roof collapsed

and the air dense with sounds
only water can understand

colonists believed the guttural growl
rushing from its air and ocean depths
was satan calling from his devil's hole

last summer humans desecrated Trott's wall
and vandalized the pool

perhaps to seek out satan in his lair

perhaps pursued by devils of their own

droning home in a somewhere direction
two bees on bikes stung me through

the blond one whose name could only be Kurt
had eyes gestapo blue

the other wearing a cause
had chrome wheels and a chrome heart too

so i scotchtaped the home tailing kite
of my fly-away hair

and zzzzooooommmmmmmm
through the hived and vibrant air
we winged highvoltaged hungry

gorging on light sound taste
sugared stars   the honeycomb night

while a psychedelic cricket played a kazoo
's all right baby
's all right
's all right
's alright

the bermudian cashier
at the parakeet
apologized for giving me change
in bermudian money

her shame caught like a chickpea
in the throat of that
mindless repetitious bird

kiskadee kiskadee kiskadee
    pursuing me

1973 recalling the crocodile
county okefenokee
a dime short the price of
deep south pecan pie

i offered 50 cents exchange
    canadian

            we don' take yo' kine
            ah shet honey
            said the cashier

apologetically i answered
    sorry

            i pride myself
            on travelling light

                the illusion of freedom
                is weightless

                it packs so easily

iv   soul fire/ black star

a surly august   then the rains came down in a soft
whiplash   the scent of bruised cedars grieving the
air   sunset   we sat the ocean's edge to watch for
the black exodus of clouds
                              sun spewing up a blood phlegm
as if torn raw from the cindered mouth of a volcano

                         but the clouds revoked their thunder
diffusing in a cirrus formation   sky's opaque blue
retina veined with long white filaments   the sun's
glare a brassy reflection gilding the waves
                                        and in that
silence nothing stirred or breathed

                         on our arrival at the cottage we felt
the ghostly fears of seamen carried to these shores
tall ships of graveyards manned by the walking dead

plastic lawn chairs heaped in pirates' bones across
the grass   parasols wound and tied in
                                   canvas   shrouds
shutters nailed and battened tight against the wind
the shredded british flag afloat the captain's roof
                                        pinned half-mast

                    suspended in a belljar the pastel
houses   the hissing geese guardians at the church
wall   Ula's blackness disembodied her white smock
a misty ectoplasm

                                        stood apart
                                        from us

and all the while the tonedeaf tree frogs sang the
same chorale

                            i thought of beethoven
searching out a lost chord

                        a hurricane of silence
                        like a knotted fist in
                                    his brain
                        clenching unclenching

above us a casablanca fan   metallic wings whirring
frantically   comes to a stop   all light and power
diminished   the fact of our presence   fingermarks
echoes footprints
                    the scooped hollows pillowing our heads
erased   we light the hurricane lamp   who and what
we were   nebulous   afloat the motherwomb of quiet
voices unsyllabled flowing the body

                        and the mind's transparency

                                        music

somewhere on the island in a back room   a portrait
of malcolm X the stark decor
                              the tail of the hurricane is
                              cutting loose   other voices
                              seeping through walls
                                        a blood amoeba
                                              changing
                                              widening

local radio announcer

riot police armed with batons
held back 500 protesters
storming the case mates prison
16 kilometers outside of hamilton
the island capital
in a last appeal for the lives of
erskine durrant burrows and
larry winfield tacklyn
            their appeal was rejected
by the colonial tribunal

burrows

me and larry tacklyn he likes me to call him by his
middle name winfield he calls me buck i like that
the leader of the black cadre anti colonialists should
have a strong name buck is a strong name better than
erskine well we went that day to the supermarket and
i was feeling real good a black song going round and
round in my head singing softly to myself and winfield
he gets right mad buck you is a stupid bastard what

for you doing this why you singing a black song a black
song don't fill your empty belly we are done with singing
hear me i hear him but i'm hungry why can't we grab
some food off the shelves smash the things off the shelves
shoot anyone quick and go home but winfield is another
kind of hungry it has to be what he wants or he don't
want it those two the two white men standing together
executives written on them fuckin' tags dammit buck are
you with me or not then winfield and me killed the
executives like we killed the police commissioner george
duckett last year and next in line is governor george
sharples and his aide de camp hugh sayers winfield my
head hurts the black song is still going round and round
in my head why are we killing and killing lately i forget a
lot but winfield always knows the answers and when he
tells me the answer it all comes back to me we are doing
this to remind everyone on the island especially the black
people of the evilness and the wickedness of colonial rule
that was 1973 we killed the supervisors if anyone wants
to know see winfield i'm remembering good and how we
shot sharples dog the great dane stone dead i only
wanted to shoot him in the legs to slow him down coming
at us i like dogs he can't help it he's colonial that's crazy
thinking buck you got to stop thinking crazy thinking
soft it ain't no way for a leader i hear you winfield singing
to myself softly you didn't catch me that time doing it

local radio announcer

the dawn execution
of erskine durrant burrows
and larry winfield tacklyn
took place friday
marking december 2 1978
as a sad day in the history
of the island
its first public hanging since 1946
        both men were buried in the
seclusion of the grey stone prison

front street shopowner

we know there were three conspirators
the third one escaped the island
i was thoroughly shocked by the public response
1200 signatures   church vigils   rallies
appealing for mercy
burrows was supposed to be the crazy one
to think that they could get away with it
tacklyn and burrows
must have both been crazy
did they consider for a moment
what this would do to tourism and to
our whole economy
        the hanging was just
we taught the blacks a lesson
they won't forget

malcolm X
the late black muslim
reigns supreme at the headquarters
of the black parliamentary opposition
the progressive labour party
where a black power movement
was made known
in late october 1970

there is no undisputed evidence
to support the view
that erskine durrant burrows
self appointed leader of the black cadre
anti colonialists
was a former member of the infant
movement modelled on the
oakland california original

numbering perhaps 120 in all
their uniform was the black beret
and black leather jackets

     they were known not to carry arms

writer margaret carter

pre election november 1980   i sit alone reading in
the vast emptiness of prospect square   at first
british military   stiff upper lips and regimental
converted to schools   not even prestigious ones
the haughty proud buildings are finally crumbling

iron rails pockmarked   windows smashed in places
        left left left right left a line of humanoids
blue suited from neck to ankles   black booted and
helmeted   ancient round feudal . . . shields and batons
. . . they march without moving   the sound of their
terrible feet filling the square   a child of 1939 i
have jackboots burned in my brain
i think of what it means
to be a bermudian

my country wears many strange faces

local radio announcer

all night riots
following the execution of burrows and tacklyn
still persist
using motorbikes and cb radios the rioters have
managed to avoid police blocks and
are covering the length of the island
directing molotov cocktail incendiaries
at property and smashing front street windows
        so far 14 stores and factories
a government building and a school have
suffered damage by fire
the supreme court building and a newspaper building
were among the major casualties

citizen 1

burrows was a child
with a child's mind

you don't hang a child
for being retarded

his crime was being born black

if tacklyn and burrows
were white men
there would have been
        no hanging

local librarian

the whole affair was overpublished
misrepresented
the canadian press in particular
look at this ridiculous picture
huge tribes
of romanian south africans
portrayed as bermudians

3500 blacks live on the island
of these only five or six hundred
took part in the riot
        you would think that canada
        a sister british colony
        would be much better informed

citizen 2

high noon tea
i was setting out the dalton china
teacups when the voice of the governor
sir peter ramsbottom came on the telly
or was it the radio
announcing the curfew 6 pm to 6 am
i expect there will be a rise
in population   all that time
and nothing to do

such a bother
shopping for groceries before curfew
everyone in a hurry   tourists underfoot

those dreadful men
the whole affair is dreadful
a positive disgrace to the island
a slight to her majesty
and the british commonwealth

citizen 3

jes' as i'm seein' you an' don' anyone tells you my
eyesight ain't loud and clear   there he was sittin'
on my doorstep right wheres that shack is holdin'
together with chicken wire same as me jeremiah there
he was the man hisself malcolm X

mind says malcolm X
all revolutions are fought over land
this is your land   your freedom land   your struggle
mind he says you make them listen

put your hand to the revolution
smash the face of white injustice
make them hear   not movin' my cane i says to him
the tail of the hurricane is upon us   god have mercy
on our souls but i'se too weary to lift my head and
i'se too smart to play with fire   remember when
pondhill was a fittin' place to live   i'se seen worse
in new yawk   for what we shall receive o lord
let us be grateful

yassah i'se got my piece of land   ain't no one
gonna fight over pondhill   and malcolm X he gave
up the ghost to do his peachin' in the court
or elsewheres the lord be praised

local radio announcer

police efforts to disperse crowds
of rioters with teargas
have not been effective
business offices in hamilton centre
were ransacked
a bus was hijacked and
driven into a wall
an incident at the southampton princess
hotel resulted in fatalities
arson by parties unknown
having no connection with the rioters
is suspected   the chamber of commerce is
advised to put up their shutters
to repel attacks from lead pipes and
flying bricks

this is larry thomas of zbm radio
continuing to keep you informed
with the latest news
on the scene

now back to the turntable
with don ho and his islanders
bringing you the beautiful sound
forever bermuda
your favourite and mine
bermuda is another world
and for all the lovely ladies out there
listening in
island girl   the song making the
nightspots

tourist

i don't know what the fuss was all about   it could
have been homeweek in dee troyt   can't see why the
hell they'd need a whole battalion   a royal regiment
of fuselliers from britain to hold down a handful of
commies   still you got to give these people credit
for putting on a great show   muscle   that's what
every country needs   less talk more muscle   yah
darn lucky for us we didn't book the southampton
escaped the fire   heard the barkeep saying some
bermudian and two american tourists died in the blaze
nothing much on tv except a cricket game   me i'm a Tiger
booster   baseball   no i can't say anything that happened at
the time of the riots spoiled our holiday   after a
shower and a change of clothes we went downstairs to

72

celebrate the curfew   rum swizzles steak and fries
can't stand foreign food   high on rum we joined the
other tourists in the street and danced till dawn

      still can't forget the hotel sky lit up like
independence day from a downtown liquor warehouse
miles away   jesus what a waste of booze

citizen 4

mark was my best friend
one of the supervisors
who was killed

the nicest thing about him
was his hair
reddish brown

he played a trumpet in
the school band

ave maria was his favourite song

it's not too far from here
just down the road
turn right until you reach
the grounds   the graves of
the governor and his aide de camp

the graves are made so no one
can desecrate the bodies
i don't know where the great dane
was buried

they were taking a stroll on the grounds
of government house
the governor took pride in his appearance
i think he was wearing
his khaki safari suit
the day he was shot down

why did they have to kill the dog
why did they have to kill mark
it's all so senseless
i can't imagine where
all that anger came from

preacher

if you recognize in me
your own dark blood
death and the resurrection
our mutual destiny
then brother   sister
join and work as one
or surely we shall hang
on the meathooks of the pharisee
and the stone you lift
to build your separate temples
that stone will fall
        on you and me

mrs lois brown-evans mp jp

we
      in the progressive labour party
. . . see heritage day
as a stepping stone to true nationhood
and eventual independence

human rights activist

colonial rule is had its day
is played out Mon'   played out

somewheres along the freedom road
we is losin' ourself

can't hear my voice   no more
is someone else talkin' for me
thinkin' for me   doin' for me
what don't need doin'

twenty years they been pushin' us
pushin' us   pushin' us down
troops   warships   riot squads
can't hold us back   no more

workin' class black gonna get his rights
bermudian gonna get his rights
      no fenced off private property
      to his own beaches   no more

hey Mon'
what you wanna do us for

we ain't goin' along with u s missiles
blastin' off our island

we ain't goin' along with none of them
who is tellin' theyselfs
they's doin' good
helpin' the lowdown nothin' black

and you my brothers
turnin' away   turnin' away
puttin' on a white face
as suits them
what place you at

people got to learn their place
or we teach them

ain't no one
gonna put hisself in my place
                    no more

liquor warehouse representative

i attribute our loss in the fire
to the forces of evil
and the antichrist

v while we slept
        and dreaming

bus shelters are citadels
buffeting bermuda gales
honeymoon couples   drydock sailors
          on first leave
          sixteen months at
                    sea

entrance concave
a small cathedral
          martin luther's bedchamber
          smelling of morality
          and mouldering
               tapestries

cocooned in humidity
time unravels slowly
my watch ticking
    sledgehammer
minutes   seconds
said 4 o'clock a hundred years
                ago

icemaiden in my mental parapet
i view the christ figure
of a citizen   arms out
          spread

martyred to a crazed tourist's
careening motorbike
      pinning him to a stone
                    wall
          across the street

this wall
uniquely bermudian
      is breached in line of
      a now rare primeval cedar
      on the property enclosed

      six inches of topsoil
      surfacing volcanic
            rock

sailor's rope
pulled through the breach
encircles the broadening
      circumference
      of the pyramidal giant
          leaves silvered
          with antiquity

riddle

is the tree holding the wall
or is the wall
holding the tree

in the leaf too little
for the flower fills it

you everywhere

a part
but insufficient
to fill my eye

i's fourth dimension
groping

to find in separateness
entirety

if putting the leaf
        the eye   the i
together

i shoulder this moment's
molecule

will the flower move
to make the world you

while we slept and dreaming

cocooned in the mothering comfort
of our camping bags

the red spores of our dayborn anxieties
evolving dream sequence into parables
a twilight sleep

the mushroom grew outside the threshold of our tent

a thick finger pointing God
primeval roots penetrating cinders   clay
the vertigo of darkness

it moved through genesis
the seven days of creation

overnight

         we stood in the drenching rain and marvelled
the tawny underside   spoked vertebrae
an umbrella of wind   a wind umbrella

and roundly like a swollen sun puffed with fluid

light as a morning pancake on the black griddle

her crown

circling a space beyond our space

        that was the mushroom summer
we gathered specimens and gently swaddled
in cotton batting
stored them on a shelf away from harm

some too delicate for human touch
disintegrated into ochre dust

or in suspension emulating death
turned to angel wings of stone

        but she   her black roots fixed
at the spasm of upheaval   a scream out of hell
hooked tendrils inward still clutching earth
her full crown

soft as an underpuff of eyelid

          holding you
against my flannel shirt
i feel a surging of black roots
from a burned out star

black asterisk the nipple of your breast
the flesh torn   uprooted   screaming

your body lightened by fluid
the same texture of her soft and nothingness

        i found no mushrooms on the island
lush   extravagant   subtropical
almost obscene in its beauty

earthwoman
wide hipped promiscuous
languidly squatting anywhere

dropping her seed with the ease of smiles
reserved for tourists

        you would have to live in my country
to know the differences
to understand
understand

the stubbornness of prairie sunflowers
seared by frost but still blooming

the rage of stunted northern trees
cleaving stone to reach a cold hard sun

the quiet violence of arctic moss
pushing through permafrost of pain

        or the terrible magic of mushrooms

a high wind lays siege on harbour city
tunnelling labyrinths of ancient passage
to the dry moat below
fort hamilton

the wind is woman here
her mad hair snaring
seedpods   spiders
dispersing them where it pleases her

splits ligaments of knotted allspice trees
topples pride of india from the sky
bamboo creaking like the raw mast of
a ship too long at sea

20 watt globes
wedged
in cracks
of
seeping
limestone
light
the
way

forty stairs
and
forty stairs
again

spacing

the coming and going
of incidental humans

my wet gumsoled shoes
imprinting like acne
smooth surfaces
of steps hewn in stone

                    muskets loaded
                    watchful positioned   peering
                    through the loophole of disaster
                    cut in the strongwall
                    each man a sentry
                    to his own death
                    anticipated the expected

overhead ramparts
bristling cannon
the albatross spanish armada
        sighted

acrid stench of gunfire
her bullheads ripped apart
canvas crumpling
hatches brimmed and sealed
dismembered bodies buoying like
bits of cork on the thrashed
        timbered waters
                leeward

it never happened

where they might have stood
the light curves in a half moon

mossy sponge of lichen
seals the gouged wound in the wall

designs   toothed spleenwort
asparagus fronds   ferned maidenhair
patterns of mutant black begonia
splotched across its face

                your shadow goes before me

            look   you say
            the dry moat garden
            is growing through
                  the wall

i guess you knew
knowing i have to travel circles
to arrive at a straight line

the slave wall enduring three centuries
(expecting the expected
something i try not to do)

finally fell in on itself

and i had to look elsewhere
to explain it

      my first time on the island
the night before departure
(i told you about it more than once)
i went to a dinner in my honour

white   polite   hosted by a mad
lady of shallott
spinning tales of iceland   her homeland
with the skeins of her golden hair

until
shorn like a nun doing penance
for crimes not yet committed

she smashed the image in her mirror
she smashed the wall

and left this place

your friend is here to take you home
she said   tell him to come up

meaning Ron   black   inconspicuous
in the shadows twelve steps below

but no one moved toward it

i hear you Lani
the slave wall was there all the time

i only needed you to remind me

bermuda black the night
my back against the slave wall

evening star's poinsettia
bursts in a calyx of light

penetrating death's skull
the blind regions of human sight

and i touch the passing of souls
that meet and cross
the star-born centuries

i am not alone

somewhere in a crevice of the slave wall stone
one blink of his eye
evolving an eternity

is lizard in his joseph's coat
circling with me
the coloured spectrum of the soul's transformation

soul fire / black star
are we not all
joined in bondage still

bearing the weight of love
and its loss

        see where the scarred black edges
of that hill
beyond the trybe road turn

the imprint of our naked feet
like sun on water burn

and a third set of footprints
together and beside us
which even as we climb
              are washed out by the tidal rain

though here below the slave wall
older than island memory can trace
the signs are plain

in the resurgence of an emerald flame

where
    healing
        the broken circle
        joins itself

my pilgrimage began
        and now ends

circles that touched
and overlapped

must journey as i

        swimming in embryo
        toward
        the light of recognition

single stars
in their aloneness

a sleeping poem
nudges my thoughts
a seagull beckons land

        the dark blue waterlilies
        of the mind
            open and close
            on tranquillity

i let the poem sleep

across spilled fields
my feet upturning churn
earth   infinite stone

the gaptoothed weeds
a hag's smiling
drop their pointed seed

suppliant   without hurry
the moon ripens

i move in her and myself
the juice of melons
                apricots

halved and almond
as the calcine stone

small scar
where the seed fell away

DEC 21 '90 C